don't wait til i die to love me

iii

Michael Tavon

other works by the author

to the readers:

after publishing, *before i die, i must say this* i said i was going to hold off on writing poetry books for a while. but after a mini hiatus, i realized how much i needed to write to keep sane. as a florida native living in connecticut, winter days can be unbearable. to negate my negative emotions, i practice yoga and sound healing, but writing will always be my therapy.

in this collection, all of my poems are timestamped and dated. most of the poems are new, but plenty of them are old. i incorporated my older poems so you can see how much i've grown as a writer and person over the years.

after reading this collection, please take the time to leave a review on amazon or goodreads. reviews are crucial to helping a book reach more potential readers.

section i

love poems

7:09 am. 11.11.21

come as you are
  not how the world wants you to be
  don't put on a front
  who you are is enough for me

come as you are
  there is no need to conceal
  show me your battle wounds
  together we will heal

you have spent years
  fighting for those
  who didn't deserve your heart
  is this why you believe love is war?

if you let me in
  i promise
  you will not be a heartbreak causality
  i will be the shelter you need
  to feel serenity.

there is no need to be alarmed
  let down your guard
  and i will give you my all
  all i ask is
  for you to come as you are

Don't Wait til I Die to Love Me III

i saw what my mother went through
with men - it wasn't pretty

as i grew into my manhood
i vowed to never make a woman's
life ugly

i tried my best
to be a good man
to all my lovers and flings
i may have broken a few hearts
along the way
but that's the way love goes
i can assure
no woman's life became ugly
because she fell in love with me
my voice never raised
my fist never swung
if i was committed to one
she never had to smell loins
to prove it

i never wanted to be like the
men my mother loved.
in a way ain't shit men
influenced me to be a good one

unspecified time. 2.10.16

i wanna fly to a perfect place

   where we can see eye to eye
   and never feel no pain,
   let me penetrate your deepest mental space
   so, i can elevate your brain
   and make you climax from the soul,

my love is pure my heart is gold

   let's fly to neverland
   so we will never grow old,
   i know this world is cold
   and people are deceiving
   they make like the fall
   when it's hard and start leaving

please believe

   when i say my lois lane
   i'm here to save the day
   no time to waste
   cause i'm already late
   how could i be fly without my suit and cape
   you take my breath away
   when we lock lips like cpr,

you are my nova, a shooting star

just know i am near
no matter how far you are my angel,
and i will always be around
to protect you from
all of the pain too

Michael Tavon

4:44 pm 1.20.22

love is the only language i speak,
when i care for you
it won't be a secret
my affection will be loud
like a marching band

i will be the pillow you need
to support your dreams
when you can't sleep

loneliness will have no
place to live.
for you, i will always be here

when i say
i love you,
believe every syllable

because my word is gospel
and love is a principle

3:46 am 2.1.22

february just arrived... we survived the heaviest snowstorm of our lives… big white hills and small cloudy mountains peak over the buried grass… we sled with our niece. how her little giggle cuts through the cold air as we descend melts my heart... and your lucent smile makes being in this -2 degree weather worthwhile...

february just arrived…winter isn't letting up anytime soon...she has something to prove this year…we'll write poems together...do yoga…drink hot beverages...read literature…play board games...and everything in between to keep our minds occupied and relationships full…

february just arrived…i'm pleased to be stuck in our warm abode with you.

1:48 AM 3.6.22

I think of you
When the moon is crescent
And the way your eyes shine
As you cherish the beautiful jewel in the sky

I think of you,
When I hear your favorite song
And imagine your heart smiling
When the lyrics spoke to you
for the first time

I think of you
When good food settles
in my belly,
You cook like a chef from heaven
It's a blessing to taste
The meals you season
With spice and everything nice

I think of you
When I use your lotion or shampoo
Then you crack jokes
because I smell like you

I think of you,
When rain falls into my hand
It reminds me of your gentle embrace

My five senses
Admire the things you do
That's why I won't stop thinking of you.

2.6.22 8:40 pm

lead me to a place i've never been,
but don't drag me through hell to get there

7:52 pm 1.31.22

we healed from past heartaches
and grew into the best of friends
we didn't leave room
for old baggage to crowd our space
we became each other's haven
for honest conversations
& fell in love with a clean slate
our home is sacred
because trust is our foundation

2:17 pm 2.1.22

(after nikki giovanni' *i wrote a good omelet*)

after a morning of loving you

i rest my head on a poem
and write a soft pillow
as i watch you put on the clothes
i had undone

i listen to the dishes
and wash my favorite songs
as you patiently wait
for your coffee to brew
o the way my body smiles
after loving you

i watch the floor,
and mop the sports news
the silly little things
i do after loving you

you spin me like a vinyl
i'm easy like lionel i moonwalk like michael

it's easy to feel the rhythm
after a morning of loving you

8:01 pm 1.31.22

how could i not trust you
from the beginning
you've exposed me to every layer of you

2.14.19

i love so hard
the ground *shakes*
when my heart beats for you

1:18 am, 1.21.22

trusting you never feels like an extreme sport. sleeping next to you is far from a nightmare. and coming home to you never feels like war. being with you is like soft ocean tide under the moonlight. with you in possession of my deepest feelings, life is secure and serene. i once believed falling in love was scary as hell, then you proved me wrong. love is a voyage that allows you to dive into the oceans inside you without drowning each other.

1.11. 16

love is a verb
  it's something you prove
  choose, gain, and lose
  it's a game for two,
  win, lose, rarely a draw

it turns pride into a fool
  it makes the kind, cruel
   not a tool, often misused

love is why we wake up
   whether we know it or not
   our undying infatuation
   is our motivation

we continue to chase
  this thing called life
  a war in which
  we earn scars and stripes
  love is why we fight
  it's what we yearn
  to sleep next to at night
  love is life

Don't Wait til I Die to Love Me III

there was a time
i thought i didn't deserve
you -

true love
eludes the hopeless romantics
who chase it -

many times i got lost
searching for love in
all the wrong places

then came you
the right person
at the right time
it's always one or the other
the wrong lovers
always knew where to find me
and time was rarely on my side

i had my reasons to doubt

not you, but me

what did i do to deserve
someone like you?

your feelings were true

and i wondered why?

i thought of the ways
i would fuck it up

in you,
i found everything i ever wanted
my first response
was to question why i was enough

Don't Wait til I Die to Love Me III

1.2.17

be my peace in a state of war
be the thread
where my heart is torn.
be the muse
when my thoughts are dull
be the sensation when i feel numb

show me your love
and i'll reciprocate it
with every breath in my lungs
together we'll grow
strong, so strong
a hurricane wouldn't
tear us apart

i can't wait to get you near, my dear.
i have a lifetime of love give
without fear.
in the meantime
stay gold and continue to grow

2.3.16

i love you
like we fell for each other
in a past lifetime

the moment you said hi
life changed
before my very eyes

2:14 pm 3.6.22

free falling with a gentle heart
often results in scars
but it makes you stronger
and void of fear
when you dust yourself off
and fall in love again

no one said this journey
would be easy,
finding the perfect one
is an extreme sport
with years of losses and lessons

remain soft
despite crash landing
time and time again

in due time,
you'll find the person
worth falling for
when they catch your descent
with hands you can trust

12:23 pm 1.27.22

my heart belongs to you
the way the sun intensifies the morning sky

my heart belongs to you
the way the night sky belongs to the moon

5:00 pm 2.3.22

i cherish the nights when we revisit the first time
we saw each other face to face --

your ear caught the drumbeat from my heart
when our bodies connected for an embrace
warmer than beach sand.

after months of longing for each other from a
distance - the moment of truth was in our
hands.

we reminisce our first kiss,
o how nerves traveled from
our guts to our lips
the raw tension made sparks fly
the butterflies in my stomach
rose like sunrise,

then you tell me
about each fluttering thought
your mind hosted leading up to
our divine moment in time

between the lust below
and the uncertainty of tomorrow
we took what we felt in the moment
and turned it into a beautiful

collision of everything
 our souls were missing

the more we retell our story
the more nuanced it becomes
i love those nights
when we cuddle in the dark
and ruminate the day
our fate was written

Don't Wait til I Die to Love Me III

3:44 pm 2.7.22

She has a way with words
painting her feelings
in beautiful prose

never speaks in riddles
her pen dances in rhythms

heart wide open
expressing her affection
in poems
—-
poetry lady, hold me close
wrap me in bare sheets
leave ink tracings
all over my soul
— —
she knows me out and in
a sculptor with a pen
she shapes me in ways
i don't even see

how fearless is she
writing to escape
she just wants to be free

the outsiders don't understand

she doesn't care
all she needs
is a pad a pen at hand
—
my poetry queen
your words - safe with me
a refuge from all the
dark that carries me

2.26.18

share your pain with me
    and i'll do the same
    we'll watch our wounds heal
  the way a broken rose
  blooms after it rains

5:00 am 2.1.22

life changed when i fell in love with you

i can be a walking headache - i'm a scatterbrain - a self-loather- sometimes i miss the grease that sits in the pots after i scrub them - i get so hooked on the PS5 i leave the trash in overnight.

you despise when i leave washcloths in the sink… but i make it all up with foot rubs and tummy massages when those cramps start to bully you...i know i'm not the easiest to live with..i'm like an oversized kid.. but you love the child in me…

to find someone like you... a spirit eager to spend the rest of your days dealing with my pisces moods - my sarcasm – and passive-aggressive ways was a blessing i didn't see coming.

my life changed when i fell in love with you because you fell in love with all of me something i never experienced before you.

7:16 pm 2.2.22

(confessional)

the turning point… the perfect stranger arrived
during my worst time…she was grieving over
the loss of her friend and dealing with her
loveless relationship ..we became each other's
safe space… as we began the journey of healing
ourselves…we were there to listen and share the
deepest feelings we only wrote in poems…she
never put the burden on me to save her… i
didn't put the burden on her to fix me… our
bond flourished because we weren't
codependent…she believed in my dreams…as i
did hers…when she cut ties her him… and i
ended all of my situationships… falling in love
with her was gentle like a drifting feather … it
felt natural…meeting her changed my life… she
became the beginning to the life i always
dreamed of.

Michael Tavon

10:48 pm, 1.29.15

each day i fall in love with you
more & more
my heart beats a tempo
you can't ignore
you remind me of a daydream
a scenic view of love and tranquility

you have all this love
never let go
our journey is a river
let it flow
this feeling is natural
like summer breeze strumming your hair
love isn't hard
when you handle with care

10:52 pm 1.31.22

you are the sunlight in my life
you aurify the dark clouds that once rained
inside me.

2.12.16

love is like water
you become weak without it
your soul gets ravenous with a passion
'til you can't breath
in bed laying with cold sweats
because you can't sleep without it

see without love
there would be no you or me
without water it would be the same thing

water and love
keeps the world spinning
despite being diseased with
famine and sinning

we were created by love
raised by water
through trial and error
love prevails, never falters
as we float the coast
to our seafoam alter
 ' o how love and water
 is what we need the most
yet we abuse the two
with little remorse

Don't Wait til I Die to Love Me III

9:56 pm, 12.23.22

when it's five below
you're the only warmth
my body knows
our bed - a refuge
from the crystal cold
as snowflakes rain on our window
the sweetest way to remind me
i'm not alone

hold me tight,
i'll do the same
let's fade into each other
the way dreams fade into day

trapped by darkness
and snowstorms
we possess endless love
in our arms
to provide enough comfort
til dawn

10.24.2015

it was hard to believe
too good to be true
i thought you were a mirage
girls like you come
once in every two lifetimes

Don't Wait til I Die to Love Me III

i go to sleep to dream about you
when i wake up, i still do
my days are pitch black
without you there are no hues

loneliness is a grey cloud
and you were my silver lining
my diamond in the sky is gone
now there is no shining

out in the cold again
while the sky is crying

i miss you when you're not here
hoping you think of me as an idea
you're gone, i'm still here

you treated me like a daydream
you let me slip from your brainwaves

you surfed and found a new way
 you're far away
my love remains
until the sky falls
and the oceans wash us away

12:05 am 1.16.22

with your gentle hand,
on my chest, it lands
the rhythm of my existence
plays a gentle song
in your palm
you handle with care
when you touch me there
i never feel alone,
i know you'll never betray
my heart

section ii

love adjacent poems

Michael Tavon

2:15 pm 2.8.22

trust is a home
often abused by
careless people
you care for

this sacred place
you've created to make others
feel safe, has become a jungle
for savages to dwell

they claim to care
but always late on rent
they treat your trust like shit
until you threaten to evict

when they finally leave
you're left with holes in the wall,
a collapsing roof and busted pipes

rebuilding this home all alone
helps you learn -
you can't let anyone in
without doing background checks

note to self

my kindness isn't for broken people to put their
burdens on. i don't mind helping the people i
care for, but not at the expense of mental health.
once i feel like i'm losing pieces of myself to save
them, letting them go will be the best option.

10:55 am 9.21.17

realizing i was empty
because i never found myself
was the best epiphany i ever had
now being alone is more blissful
than ever.

i no longer yearn for love from
another heart as heavy as years before
because i've finally learned
how to love myself.

Don't Wait til I Die to Love Me III

5:20 AM 3.20.22

Because we're young
We spend our days
Like we have an endless supply of time

Always waiting for the perfect moment
to do what the heart desires
Without realizing
we're living on borrowed time
- nothing is guaranteed

Youth is fleeting,
The more we sit back
And wait for the right time
The more regrets we will create
before we die

Make the big leap,
Follow your dreams -
Tell the people you love
how you feel
& Travel the world
While the hands of Father Time
Still prays for you

This life only belongs to you
For a brief period

Michael Tavon

Own it - seize the day
When you grow old
You'll be proud of the
Life you made

message:

i am my own home
i will learn to love the warmth
inside me

7:00 am 2.1.22

roses are futile at funerals
i believe in giving flowers when
the person can still smell the petals fresh.

my pride will not imprison my tongue
to prevent me from showing
the love you deserve
while you still roam the earth

how i feel will
be as translucent as ocean water
our bond will not falter
to words left unsaid

as long as you are alive
you will have a friend - so true
i will not wait til you die
to show how much i love you

Don't Wait til I Die to Love Me III

8:19 am. 1.15.22

my mood swings on a pendulum
i'm fine for one hour,
then i feel nothing,
trying to find balance
while losing my mind
i smile to hide behind

the gloom,
i wish this season
would end soon
lost in the fog
the longest winter my soul
has ever known

snowflakes dissolve like tears
anxiety manifest into fears
my heart doesn't want to be here

i'm trying, trying to find
all the bright places
inside me again.

o how the cold makes me feel alone
despite being loved at home

winter blues,
dark hues blanket the sky

Michael Tavon

this season will soon pass
i pray the sunshine will last
when it comes back

9:00 am 2.2.22

when you know your destination fight the urge
to drive down memory lane. the past is a road
you've traveled too many times before. there's
no reason to waste gas going back to the place
you've outgrown.

i had to survive my darkest nightmares to see
my dreams come to light.

9:26 pm 2.3.22

i'm married to my bliss,
no one will break us apart
i'd rather cut loose ends
before getting a divorce.

leave me alone
if my bliss makes you livid
keep your bleak energy
my soul is too vivid

9:38 am 2.3.22

for the past few years the universe has been
trying to tell me to slow down. stop getting high
off the past and drunk on the tomorrows ahead.
stay sober in the present and appreciate my
blessings today. life is too lovely to overdose on
the memories long gone and out of reach. after
being hard-headed for so damn long, i'm ready
to take heed to the wisdom the universe has
given me. my time is now, i'm ready to claim it.

Don't Wait til I Die to Love Me III

10:17 am, 1.15.22

i run the mallet along the rim
to feel the vibrations
run down my spine
i close my eyes and repeat
this moment is mine

the frequency of my singing bowl
brings back me home
when i feel lost.
a song of self-love
to reassure it takes strength
to be soft

when anxiety lifts me
off the ground
the sound of its crystal voice
brings me back down

i breathe in, exhale
allow my chakras to expand
declutter my thoughts
the power is my hand

as an overthinker
being in the present is a rarity
when the crystal bowl sings to me
i feel a moment of clarity

10:27 am 1.31.22

when was the last time
you stared into the mirror
and thanked your reflection
for existing?

how often do you set the timer to
remind yourself - you matter?

when's the last time
you exhaled a sigh of relief
and congratulated
yourself for breathing fresh air?

life is a precious gift, and your presence
is a blessing - keep on giving.

some days may seem like a losing battle
when you struggle to rise out of bed

but you are worthy
you deserve to be here
even when you're worn down

don't forget to thank yourself
for never giving up

Don't Wait til I Die to Love Me III

11:11 am, 1.20.22

as motivation exits my flesh
emptiness begins to fill me with misery
a hallowed lonely mess
i feel nothing,
amid the dusk of sky
daylight departs before i get
the chance to say goodbye

silent chaos roaring
through my mind
the rabbit hole of sorrow
is too wide to walk around
i have no choice but to free-fall down
and pray for the best

these days,
hope is a tight rope
i slackline for survival
with the wind pushing my back
and all odds against me
i take it one step at a time

one step forth is all i can promise
to the universe,
the past can be such a flirt
i refuse to look back
i'll keep fighting
despite mercury retrograde
kicking my ass

3:04 am 2.8.22

your heart knows when it's time to move on but you struggle to let go - you hold hope in the cup of your palms like water - you're too afraid to move forward - hope will spill through your fingertips if you slip. just because the past is what you know doesn't mean it's the life you should settle for.

affirm:

i am willing to work on my toxic traits. i am
willing to admit my wrongs. i will break the
cycles i constantly find myself lost within. i'm
ready to open my eyes to the truth.

11:56 am. 12.29.21

after the cold silence of struggle
amid the crossfire of self-doubt and anxiety
with battle wounds from a broken heart
grief found a home
where love once resided
i survived,
a soldier
with purple heart honors
i am
now, i speak a language of love
my mind found hope as its shelter
and bliss flows through my veins

2:44 pm 1.31.22

my heart is too forgiving to a fault. after giving
someone the benefit of the doubt, i allow them
to cross my boundaries time and time and again.
i tend to gloss over their red flags to see the best
in them. one thing about me, once i decide to cut
you off there's no chance of mending our
differences. i don't believe in rebuilding bridges
once they've been burned down.

"once i say everything
you need to hear
i won't waste another breath
over-explaining myself
my message is loud and clear."

12:48 pm 2.10.22

letting them go isn't a sign of weakness when
they become a burden to your peace. moving on
is a white flag when love becomes war. you fight
so hard to survive this battle until realizing
you're fighting alone. letting go of someone you
love requires more strength than you'll ever
know. and moving on takes more courage than
you thought you had. starting over makes you
the soldier who survived the war before it killed
you.

4.2.18

the devil loves when you self-loathe
it pleasures his dark soul,

when he sees your
hope slowly burning away
like the fire pit, in which he lays
he laughs at your pain

you scream and run
but only find
his red stare
lurking amid the shadows

he feeds off fear
with teeth, wet of blood.
he doesn't chase
he waits for you give up.

please keep running
keep throwing punches
this will be the difference
between eternal darkness
and lucid sunlight
fight for your life.

Don't Wait til I Die to Love Me III

tonight, i cried
but my tears were
as warm as raindrops
on a sunny day.

as i allowed my smile
to illuminate this cold dark room
i saw hope for the first time
in the dismal abyss.

i once accepted an old fate
the fate that said
there was no escape
and i would spend

the rest of my days
bitter. poor. alone
then i saw a sliver of light
and cried tears of hope

now i know to climb
even if it's an inch per day
until my trembling hands
touch the wet soil

Michael Tavon

until i feel the sun
 beaming on my back
up is the only way to go
so, tonight i cried
because i finally
have a reason to smile.

2:58 pm 1.31.22

there's no coming back to the person you once
knew, because by the time i let you go i've
already evolved into someone you will never get
to love.

Michael Tavon

4:44 pm 1.29.22

reminiscing is a dangerous game,
reflecting on situations, you can't change
wishing everything remained the same
blinding flashes of sadness
stun your eyes when you realize
life doesn't work that way

moving on makes you feel alone
because it forces you
to leave your comfort zone
it's time to let go

set your heavy heart free
stop clinging on
if you keep running to the past
you'll be stuck
with wasted time you won't get back

Don't Wait til I Die to Love Me III

6:23 pm 1.25.2022

(while listening to *take me home* by phil collins)

it's been so long
since i've been running
still don't know what from
i found my peace
far from home

i don't want you to miss me
just know i'm doing fine
save your worry
for the homeless dying outside

i've found my joy
don't know how long it will last
i will savor it in my hands
like snowflakes in blades of grass

the season is long,
it's blistering cold
soon after i awaken
the sun goes
here comes darkness
outside my window

but i'll be fine,
this feeling shall blow by

i'm no prisoner,
home is my life
i'm just eager to go back outside

7:00 pm 7.7.20

what if i told you
your smile will be restored
your heart will mend
after breaking down -

what if i said
the grass will grow greener
after the storm

what if i told you
pain is a fading moment
like each minute of the day
would you believe me
if i told you these things?

i hope so,
'cause change is like magic
you won't see it
if you don't believe it

6:23 pm 2.2.22

my optimism saved me from
from my darkest hour
that sliver of light
provided the hope i needed
to believe brighter days were ahead

Don't Wait til I Die to Love Me III

6:46 pm 2.2.22

i know what it's like
to work tirelessly
for the life you want
and still fall short of it all

i know what it's like
to give your
heart to the world
and feel empty
after receiving nothing in return

i know what it's like
when the struggle feels
like an achilles heel
holding you back
from your happiness

i know what's it like
to think of ways to cease breathing
because the afterlife
just makes more sense

i've been there,
but today i'm here to tell you
it gets better -
feed your heart the love you deserve
even when the sun

inside you doesn't shine

i've been where you are
i'm here to say
your life doesn't have to
stay this way.
there's always a chance
for better days

Don't Wait til I Die to Love Me III

6:55 pm 1.20.2022

when the ground is out of reach
and the clouds are under me
a new perspective is born
life and its baggage
becomes small -
why does my heart worry at all
when yesterday fades
the way earth does
when i'm on a plane

2:49 pm 1.22.22

you don't want to be the person who never
admits to being wrong, then question why the
same mistakes keep reoccurring in your life.
have the awareness to know when you're wrong
and have to humility to admit it. once you
realize you're not always right, you'll provide
more space within your mind to learn the
lessons you need to acquire to grow into a better
version of yourself.

7:06 pm, 1.20.22

don't let your pride be the reason you refuse to
apologize when you know you're wrong. have
the humility to know when it's time to set your
ego to the side to do what's right. acknowledge
the pain you caused before you burn a bridge
you won't have access to cross again.

7pm 2.10.22

i know how to apologize when i'm wrong. my
ego isn't swelled; my empathy is a well deep
enough to pour oceans into. i won't gaslight you
into second guessing yourself. there is growth in
failures, there is healing within mistakes. when
i'm wrong i will never hesitate to ask how can i
learn from it.

7:11 pm, 1.20.22

regrets are too heavy to carry - i leave them
behind. i turn my losses into lessons and watch
them manifest into blessings. i don't dread new
beginnings. there's no need to hold onto
something that will stress me out and slow me
down. i navigate life with light luggage, because
i don't stuff regrets in my briefcase. yesterday's
burdens won't hold me back. i travel to my
destination without staring in the rearview.

7:21 pm 1.20.22

there's no need to hide
the stress in your eyes
it's okay to cry

you've been working tirelessly
you fight against the daylight
and come home at night

with very little time
to decompress
between shifts,
you've become everything you fear

payday is nothing to celebrate
you're broke again, the next day
a prisoner at work
your freedom is home

you do the best you can
to make the best of it all

you know there's more to life
than this but don't know where to go

stuck in a hamster wheel
hoping enough life remains

to change —
before you grow too old to try

you deserve rest
& you deserve to pursue
the life you dream of

7:35 pm 1.20.22

treat your body with rest, spoil your mind with relaxation. there's no reward for working until your body breaks down. the more you rest, the more time you'll have to pursue your endeavors. don't allow this 'no sleep' culture to make you feel like you're falling behind for recharging your body and mind. sleep is a massage for the tired body and stressed mind. rest is productive. rest is revolutionary.

note to self:

worry less about the factors you can't control.
release yourself from the prison of expectations.
allow your passions to flow like an ocean. create
the love you deserve, don't force it.

7:44 pm, 1.21.22

as time moved on, so did i. the grudges i once
held captive have been released from their
shackles. they served no purpose for my growth,
so i set them free. i no longer possess bitter
feelings towards you; i thank you for teaching
the lessons you did through heartache. thanks to
you, i became a better lover and a stronger
person. my story would not have been the same
without the chapter you penned with me.

7:53 pm 1.20.22

i knew change was gonna come,
it could've warned me
beforehand
a moment in time
that went by too fast
i wish i could've said goodbye
before being left in the past

Michael Tavon

affirm:

i will express my feelings without shame
i will communicate my thoughts,
with confidence. my feelings and thoughts are
valued, and i would be doing my heart a
disservice by silencing my truth just to keep
others satisfied.

note to self:

i can't fix everything, and i can't be the hero
who saves everyone. sometimes it's just the way
it is, and they are the way they are. i will save
my heart a lifetime of grief once i realize i've
done everything in my power to inspire change,
i must allow the universe to do its work, and let
the cards land wherever they fall.

2.1.22 8:26 pm

some friendships
  are like a good netflix series
  easy to get attached to
  but only built to last
  for a few seasons

when friendships get canceled
  the way our favorite shows do
  you're stuck with memories
  repeating in your mind like old episodes,

a deep sadness overcomes you
  when you realize your only option
  is to let go because trying to capture
  the chemistry twice is a waste of time

11:09 pm 1.31.22

the home i've built
 since cutting ties with depression
 is filled with felicity

i do not welcome his negative energy
the door remains closed
when he visits me

i'd rather be misery's enemy
than to rehash old memories
to make him feel comfortable
in my new sanctuary

depression is part
of the past
i would never allow
 into my home again

Michael Tavon

11:12 pm 1.25.22

(after that, one episode of *this is us*
when jack lost his mother)

i thought about my mom
& the day her eyes will
shut tight like the casket
with her will lay to rest in
her eulogy came to me

it said:
when i moved away
to pursue a happier life
the life i couldn't find
at home -
she would call every week
to talk about every fleeting thought
passing through her mind
sometimes the conversations were general
 like the weather or pandemic stuff –
other times our conversations
became therapy sessions
my mother -
introduced me to versions of her
i wasn't privy to
she discussed her heartaches,
postpartum depression, aspirations, regrets
see, under one roof

we'd go for days
without speaking much
we tiptoed around our feelings
which often created tension
we talked about
money, bills, dinner, and tv shows

moving away made us closer
sometimes those conversations
lasted well over an hour,
as she expressed every passing thought
i was on the other side
trying to find the right time
to say, "goodbye, i love you."

she spoke a mile a minute
trying to cram every word
in between to leave no space
for me to say goodbye

now, as i stand here
i just want one more call
this time
i let her speak until she falls asleep
because i don't want to say goodbye

i'm thankful
my mother introduced me
to the parts of her
i yearned to know growing up

it helped me understand why

she loved the way she did

because of those phone calls
i got to know
the happy version of her,
the healed version of her,
the real version of her.

as time went on my appreciation
for those long calls grew,
even though i tried to rush
her off the phone.
every now and then

i'd give anything to hear,
"all right, baby, talk to you soon. love ya."
 one last time.

11:23 pm 1.29.22

if i could travel back in time and have a
conversation with my seventeen-year-old self, i
would say:

 your dreams are too vivid for reality. that's why
your peers try to dim your light for living with
your head in the clouds. break out of your shell
show the world how unique you are. never hold
shame for being you. those who mock your
passion only belittle you to make themselves
feel larger. you may not see it now, but being
misunderstood will be your greatest blessing.
your journey was tailor-made for you, you were
not born to follow suit. do not stress about
fitting in. being misunderstood will pay off
when you travel in your own lane.

affirm:

i am (a) present - wrapped in gold
a gift to behold
appreciate my worth
or leave me the fuck alone

note to self:

your smile will shine brighter when you stop
living for others and start building the life you
envision for yourself.

11:44 pm, 1.29.22

i discovered joy when i stopped concerning
myself with how others perceive me. i refuse to
shapeshift into a version of me to please anyone.
i'm not rude, but don't push me. i will never go
out of my way to cause harm or drama, and i'm
too lowkey for confrontation. you not liking me
is an outcome i can live with.

1:11 am 1.28.22

as i shed old flesh
and bloom into a better version of me
i say farewell to the fears of yesterday
and the gloomy thoughts of tomorrow
today i am where i need to be,
i won't fixate on the elements
i can't control,
i owe myself a clean slate
i deserve to give myself a second chance
i am not a failure for the mistakes
made in the past
i am wise because of them

message:

the more i grow the more i appreciate the
mistakes i made in my youth. without them, i
wouldn't be as wise as i am today.

1:36 am, 1.21.22

once you cost me peace, it won't be long before i
realize you're no longer worth spending energy
on. i refuse to go emotionally bankrupt on
people who don't see the value in loving
themselves. if you only enter my life to drain me
with drama and chaos, i will choose my joy over
you every single time.

note to self:

your affinity for helping others will lead you
into becoming a refuge for broken souls if you
don't set healthy boundaries. protect your peace,
don't let them take advantage of you.

2:57 am 1.20.22

life is messy,
a clusterfuck of madness
where clarity is a lost treasure,
and love is a dying art
no one leaves unscathed
that's the beauty of it all
as time blesses us with
grey hairs, wrinkles, and scars
we learn to appreciate
this messy life of ours
because we realize how
precious it is
to be alive

3:01 am 1.23.22

when waves of self-doubt and sadness come
crashing down, may the words you speak upon
your heart be gentle like a sea breeze. recognize
the power in your voice when speaking to
yourself the way your treat your heart will
become the manifestation of your reality. affirm
your greatness when those relentless waves try
to drown you. save yourself by loving yourself.

4:01 am, 1.05.22

cry the way rain pours,
when dark clouds release
their sorrow,
be the storm
that inspires new life
when the sun shines
for a brighter tomorrow
don't hold in your hurt
allow your tears to flood
your past,
you'll see destruction when
you think about going back

4:56 am 1.27.22

after working on yourself for so long
 find the light to smile inside & out

you've been so patient
crafting the best
version of you

celebrate your milestones
even if you're still far from finished

note to self:

i am not solely defined by my past.
my heart is a conglomerate of all the experiences
i have grown from. i am proud of all the battles
i've fought. i will continue to push through
every obstacle the universe places in front of me.
i will never stop healing.

note to self:

some people get so bitter when they see you win
but fail to acknowledge the obstacles you had to
overcome on your way to the finish line.

section iii:
something like love poems

2/26/22

when life changes
flow with the waves
never go against the ocean
you will drown
if you fight to keep
currents those flowing
in the same direction
real growth happens
when you embrace change

1:11 pm 1.26.22
(proud uncle poem)

the love from a toddler
- pure and warm
when they're excited to see you
they run into your arms

the moments when they rest
their head on your shoulder
you yearn for these moments
to never be over
but you can't stop them
from getting older

their uncontrollable laughter
when you tickle their tummy
enriches your soul more than
any amount of money could

o how their happy feet
tap dance on the floor
when you play their favorite song
precious and carefree,
in their eyes
you could do no wrong

being loved by a toddler
makes life so worth it
on the days you feel down
they give you purpose

12:41 pm 1.26.22

to the father,
imperfect but present
you taught me patience
through hours angling
and chess matches

to the man who sings off-key
to the tune of his own songs
with a shameless sense of humor
you're never too embarrassed to laugh
at your own jokes

you never required
much to be content
a trait i wish i inherited from you

you, a carefree being
you were never close friends
with sobriety
while i grew up attached to the hip
with anxiety,

no fault of yours
i was born this way.

you were a happy drunk,
a sleepy one too.

Don't Wait til I Die to Love Me III

i was luckier than a lot of kids
who was raised by a drunk dad

you gave me laughter and fun memories
never a black eye

we played catch and hopped together
i never had to hide under
my blankets at night
I regarded you as my hero,
a man i never had to fear
a deadbeat you couldn't be
you were always near

a simple man
who lives a simple life
who finds joy in all the simple things

my father is the dad
most young boys dreamed of

3:58 am 2.1.22

i don't have it in me to hate someone
for loving who they love.

if he loves him or if she loves them

who am i to judge
you won't see me spewing
scriptures from a book i've never read

how can i hate someone for loving
how they were born to love?
you won't catch me cursing
them to go to church
when i haven't been to
one since the last funeral

i'm no homophobe
i'm not a hypocrite either

i believe love is equal
who people sleep with
is none of my business

everyone deserves
to love who they want
on this hell called earth

1.6.18

i can't sleep with these
tears in my eyes
voices telling me to end it all tonight
maybe they're right
i mean little to the people i love
an afterthought i've become
balancing hope on a tightrope
while holding steak knives
looking down, from up high
at my demise

people don't know the
angst lying inside
so i pretend
to be numb to the pain
when i'm soft
like a drop of rain
i splatter when i fall

now these thoughts
are stronger when sober
and i have no one to call
i'm all alone
a feeling i should be used to

5:55 pm 11.11.18

happiness is like rainfall
in the desert
and it rarely pours
but i pray every night
for a shower
to resurrect the flowers
that have turned to dust and stone

and that's hope
when your surface has become
dry and filled with dirt
you still envision
the green plants
pink flowers
towering trees
and animals prancing
on the terrain.

Don't Wait til I Die to Love Me III

4.6.18

i've learned how to turn

grief into a smile

because i didn't want

you to suffer too.

Michael Tavon

2:22 pm 1.23.22

some relatives won't
be around to celebrate birthdays
but will show up for your funeral
with wet eyes

-

consumed by guilt
because they waited til it was too late
to love you-

Don't Wait til I Die to Love Me III

4:56 pm 1.23.22

new music doesn't hit the same

the music ma & pa
grew up on still feeds my old soul
it looks like vibrant colors,
leather shoes,
feels like summer, rain,
& the love we all dream of
& sounds like something
we will never capture again

the music my big cousins grew up on
made being in the hood seem
like the place to be
it's was loud - raw
baggy clothes
mouth full of golds
a fuck you to the system

the music i grew up on
give me rhythm and a soft heart
staring through the window of our culture
106 & park
exposed me to visual art

Michael Tavon

that became timeless
in my eyes

the music today
is rehashed garbage -
reheated vibes from the past,
and shit that spoils
after a few weeks on the charts

don't get me wrong,
tons of songs have a special
place in my heart
but a lot of music today
doesn't have a spark
it's lacking something

new yeezy is meh
new drake is okay
even weezy is still good
but his old shit still gets heavy play

& many new rappers are either carbon copies of
yesterdays greats or manufactured puppets
to appeal to the youth of the today

music today don't hit the same

6:59 am 3.26.18

all alone
in a room full of lies.
sweat covered hands
and eyes filled with cries

the walls are closing
running out of breath
you've convinced yourself
you don't need help
a lie you will protect til death.

your friends
your family
miss your laugh
the old you has left
and is long gone.

"please come home"
your heart cries
instead, you please
the voices in your mind

before you pull the trigger
swallow those pills

submerge underwater.
gash your wrist

please think about the love
you will be leaving behind.
don't do it!
seek help

7.6.18

alcohol and drugs
are here to make
you feel less alone
like the old flame
you run to when there's nowhere to go
you can always count on
gin
brown
whiskey
tequila

just like the person who tore you apart
it's a toxic bond
you're afraid to let go of
you'd hate to face your problems
sober and alone

Michael Tavon

so many young souls go numb
chasing a euphoria that never comes

trying to balance their lows with highs
until they come back down to reality

no matter how far they run
there's no escaping the demons
that chase them

drugs don't negate the darkness,
you won't find peace in pipes and pills

just cheap thrills and what-ifs
even the next moment is uncertain

you're hurting, but you don't deserve to die
there's no shame in crying with sober eyes

drugs won't heal your broken heart

7.2.18

poison is pleasure in disguise
it comes in many forms
and easy to over-indulge.

you consume with no regard
using it to cope
with your angst

it makes you smile
it makes you free
it makes you forget
but it's all temporary

once that poison
settles in your stomach
it becomes a part of you
you become part of this substance
which makes it harder to let go

by the time the pleasure fades
you've come to find
pain piercing your heart again.

your toxic habit
doesn't help you cope
it only holds you back from healing.

7:57 pm 2.8.22

loving an addict is a tug of war battle

how long do you pull before
you lose the strength to hold on

the conflict between letting go to save yourself
or fighting to save them
bares a strain too heavy for most hearts
to carry

you can't help someone who doesn't want to
help themselves,

but the guilt trip will last for a thousand miles if
you create distance between you and them

only you know when to keep fighting and when
to let go

9.3.18

goodbye to
the ghost who taunted me
when i had nowhere to go

goodbye to the ghost
who found me
as i dwelled in self-pity

the ghost who tortured my soul
when i yearned for a love
not designed for me

the ghost who once gazed
over my low shoulders
laughing as i sulked
in my own anxiety

goodbye to the ghost
who was once my only friend
goodbye to the ghost
who lived inside my head

the ghost who whispered

bad advice at night

it's time to say goodbye
to the ghost
so i can move on
and fulfill
my purpose in life

4:38 am 2.1.22

amid snowfall and blue wind... i feel
like a child all over again. as soft crystals
gracefully descend from the sky...my feet sink
into the ground... it feels like i'm walking on
clouds...where i'm from, we don't get much cold
wind under the palm trees... i used to go to the
beach in january...the change of seasons is a
beautiful reminder of how much life can change
when you take a leap of faith...

2.3.22 3:33 am

when you cross the line
between platonic and romantic
you take the chance of
gaining a soulmate
or losing a friend

a gamble with so much at stake
so much to lose - even more to gain

you can play it safe
by keeping your feelings at bay
as time passes, those feelings
evolve into silent pain
inside you're fighting
to keep things the same

or you can go all in -
and say -

"everything beautiful
is synonymous with your name
when i picture
the next ten thousand days,

Don't Wait til I Die to Love Me III

Your face is in the frame."

maybe they'll reciprocate
those feelings too,
maybe they'll say
"i love you,
but not the way you want me to."

when platonic relationships
get complicated,
what do you
fall back or hope
they love you too?

6:19 pm 7.29.20

denial becomes your best friend
when the truth turns into
your greatest enemy,
as your ears combat
the words you
refuse to hear

once the news is confirmed
the truth starts to sink in
like a broken boat lost at sea
suddenly you find yourself drowning
in your own tears,
reaching for comfort,
each breath becomes more important
as you swim to shore

then you attempt
to negotiate with god
hoping you can convince him
to give that person a contract extension,
god denies your pleas and cries

because you're afraid to sleep alone,

anger finds a new home
inside of you
once your mind spirals
into thoughts of remorse
wishing you could've done more
but it's not your fault,
fate is never late to its appointments

when then the truth comes back,
you listen to its words,

despite the hurt
you laugh about the good times
and smile when the epiphany strikes

they'll be fine
in the next lifetime
and you two will meet again

1:25 pm 7.30.20

when the oxygen in your lungs
suddenly decides it no longer
wants to stay,
you're left reaching for it to comeback
as it slips from your fingertips

the hands on the clock cease to move
and time stands still
nothing feels real
as you beg the hours
to console you
but they're just as sad as you are

your heart drums
a rhythm so heavy
you stumble as you walk
because the weight is too hard to carry

your mind goes haywire
trying to process the news
you break a fuse,
yours tears learn how to away too
your vision becomes distorted

behind the mist
in disbelief,
you rub them like you're performing

Don't Wait til I Die to Love Me III

a magic trick
that will make everything reappear

sadly, you can see it, feel it
hear it, and even smell it
no matter what
your senses can never process
of how natural death is

3:39 pm 2.3.22

be mindful of how you treat people
karma isn't frugal when it comes to payback...

you can have
a life of abundance
or years of misfortune.
your actions determine
your fate

note to self:

once i learned the power of the tongue, i began
to only speak words of love to myself. i'm more
aware of the power of manifestation. even when
disappointed, i make the conscious effort to not
pity myself.

Michael Tavon

1:47 am 1.5.22

i realize
how much power my words have,
so i speak with tenderness
when talking to others
i am more aware of the messages
i put out into the universe

when talking to myself
i swim in gratitude,
instead of drowning in sorrow
when something doesn't go my way

i celebrate others when they win
opposed praying for their downfall

karma will bless me abundantly
when she pays a visit

2:38 am 1.22.22

i could've been cursed
with a sloppy drunk mother
  my ma's been sober
   her entire life.

the universe could've cursed me
 with an abusive father:
  the only tears he gave were
  from episodes of laughter.

a lazy mother could've raised me:
  giving up isn't in her blood,
  she even works in her sleep

an absent father could've deserted me:
   my pops always hooped with me
   when he got home from work.

my mother could've been loveless
with no remorse:
   it's hard for her to let her children go,
   even when they grow.

my father could've stolen my youth:
 the child inside me still lives.

my parents, deeply flawed humans
who made the best with what they had

i don't hold any grudges for their mistakes
they always had
my best interest at heart

out all of the parents
i could've had,
i am grateful to be blessed
with two who supported
and always worked
tirelessly for their children

Don't Wait til I Die to Love Me III

2.6.17

anxiety is the bridge
you must cross to feel bliss
on the other side
this bridge is often vacant
because most refuse
to cross their fears.
are you one of those people, too?

9:43 pm 2.1.22

me at 17:

i was unsure of myself
i felt like an outcast in my own skin
--hiding in a shell,
because i was embarrassed
to be myself

anxiety was my body language
and it spoke fluently when it needed
to be silent

---hives formed continents on my skin
 & my hands shuddered like
   a bad engine

confidence and i never
saw eye to eye
we fought like an
old sour couple

---the person you see today,
   didn't always walk-talk-think
   this way

i took years of digging deep
to discover the gold
that was lost within me

self-love is a journey, not a vacation

10:10 pm 2.3.22

i was taught to never judge a person for their
mistakes without understanding their
circumstance. it's easy to say what you would've
done when you're on the outside looking in, but
pressure has a way of making us break in ways
we thought we were strong. when you're back is
against the wall and a choice has to be made,
what would you do?

Don't Wait til I Die to Love Me III

1:29 am 1.24.22

the saddest part
about having a big family
is realizing the many funerals
i will attend as time slips away from us
i hope my heart is strong enough
to deadlift so much grief

4:36 pm 1.23.22

my family,
rough around the edges
soft in the middle

we show love by reminiscing,
and dancing sorrow away

uncles, aunts, cousins
grow apart with age
it's hard to keep up
with a dozen aunts & uncles
& 100 n somethin' cousins
i struggle to remember
some of their names

but we spare hard feelings
when we see each other
at rare family functions

all the smiles and hugs
helps us forget the distance
between us -

no lost love, just lost time
when we gather
we love each other

Don't Wait til I Die to Love Me III

like nothing else matters
because in the end
all we have is family
and family is all that matters

2.6.22 4:13 am

make believe confidence
my ego performs magic tricks

i've worked too hard to come this far
my heart tells me i don't belong

i'm outside the in crowd
whispers of doubt scream loud

what if my doubts are prophecies
and i'm only a jester posing as a king

7:13 pm 2.22.22

(confessional)

my lowest point...in my mid-twenties...living in ma's garage...no car...commuting on filthy public transit to my low paying job at the ymca...$9 an hour...20 hours a week...i never celebrated paydays... i knew the check would barely cover the mounting overdraft fees.. my phone service was off...the woman i loved decided i wasn't enough... i didn't blame her for choosing her future over my shitty life...my books were hardly selling...i fell for another woman but she was a young druggy with a life more hectic than mine...another woman came into my life.. i thought she was the one until her ex asked for a 20th chance... my love life was a mess... sleeping with woman after woman felt better than being lonely...i was like a car without brakes... no control of where i was headed... no sense of direction...
lost in clouds of weed smoke...i drank liquor til my stomach turned...when i say i know what it's like to feel like nothing..this is what i mean...even when i felt worthless...there were pockets of hope keeping me alive

section iv:
opposite of love poems

2.4.22 9:27 pm

i'm sorry we didn't work out
my heart was in no shape
to give you more of me

when our situation got too heavy
i pushed you away instead of
lifting you up.

my thoughts were crowded
i needed space -
i chose to fade away

maybe
you were too good for me
and i was too afraid
to fall in love with you

8:02 am 2.1.22

note to an old friend:

i'm sorry you had to let me go before you were
ready, but i promise i did what was best for
us...in the moment it seemed selfish for me to
leave when you needed me most... i couldn't
provide what you needed from me...we're
growing in different directions. we needed more
space to bloom as far as we could... moving on
was the best choice for me.. and letting go was
the only option for you.

7.10 pm. 2.4.22

it wasn't my intention
to pour pain into your heart
instead of giving you peace of mind
i caused an internal war

it's not your fault,
don't bare any blame
instead of honesty
i caused a mental strain

you wanted more than i could give
i left you with nothing at all
i became a ghost when we got close
i'm sorry for being closed off

Michael Tavon

3.2.18

loneliness is
a hollow hole

  i fill with sorrow and drugs
  crushed by your numbing love.

i get high to escape
i get high to erase
but when i come down
i fall right back into the same place

  the hollow hole
  you gashed through my aorta.

i'm feeling colder without your touch
because you were my drug
but i'm strong enough to forgive
because i miss your love.

although your deceit
is what lured me in
i'd fall for it all over again
just to caress your skin

despite replacing my bed with his
i'll be around
to let you know
my undying infatuation
would never die.

Don't Wait til I Die to Love Me III

i refuse to subside like a low tide
my eyes spread as wide as fire
when i catch a glimpse of your smile

i miss the way you say my name
i miss the way you rub my chin
i'm willing
to bury my shame
just to have you again.

i'll apologize for your mistakes
i will suppress my disdain
to be in the comfort of your warm embrace.
your grace, you left without a trace
all i have left are the fading memories
you left astray.

   but will i let them die?
   hell no not i
   i would rather dwell in our past
   than ponder our present

since you vanished
i'm suffering from the feeling of severance
but my heart is still here
waiting for the void to be filled.

3.2.18

you're like the moon
only present when dark
providing comfort
as i rest my dreamin' eyes
and weary body.

the moment i wake
you vanish like a swift wind
as the sun smiles through the blinds
i still find myself reaching
for you.

in my half-empty bed
i anticipate your arrival.
i spend my day fantasizing
your scent, your touch,

i count down the hours
minutes and seconds
until you arrive
undressed in my presence

you give me all of you
but only half the time
i'll settle for a part-time love
it's better than nothing
at all

2.16.2022

i never knew
how resilient i was
until the day you tried
to break me
i didn't crack
i became stonger

3.9.18

you come as you please
and leave nothing
but the traces of your
body on my bed

i shut my eyes
to imagine
the last kiss we shared
before you drifted away.

1.2.19

we enjoy being lonely together
we're obsessed with the feeling
of tenderness
but afraid of falling
for someone new
so we enjoy these moments
knowing that's all they'll ever be.
we think this is the easy route
but soon, we'll see how heart-wrenching
this love affair will end.

10.31.20

some people wear masks to cover the
insecurities mocking them when they glance at
their flawed reflection

others shield their face behind masks to hide
their lying eyes from the hopeful souls they gaze
upon

others wear masks to feel secure in a world
eager to tear their heart apart the moment they
expose their scars

others may wear masks
to muster the courage
to save the world around them
people wear masks for many reasons
under the guise of fun and sin
to evade the truth
like a crooked politician

whether it be
fear,
insecurities,
manipulation,
or
protection
we wear masks
to hide who we truly are,
it's ironic

we celebrate
a day of pretending
to be something
we wish we could be
'cause we hide from
the truth year 'round

8:44 pm 2.8.22

when death claims me
like a lost possession
i hope my life is something
worth reverence

i hope i've planted life into this world
i don't wanna leave this green earth starved

when death claims me
i hope i'm found fulfilled and proud
i don't want to die of a broken heart
or strangled by regret

when death claims me
i hope i'm light and free

i don't want to die
a heavy death
i want to leave my burdens behind
before soaring off into heaven

Don't Wait til I Die to Love Me III

12.9.17

in case i die soon
please tell me you love me, too

i need to know the truth
before my spirit fades into the sunset

don't hold it in today
tomorrow may not exist

yesterday is dead
and all we have is this moment.

don't waste it
biting your tongue,

tell me what i need to hear before
i disappear, say you love me, too

7:56 pm 8.12.20

this cruel world will try to make you feel weak
for caring, but it takes a great deal of strength to
love in a hopeless place. love is a superpower.

Don't Wait til I Die to Love Me III

8:48 pm 9.24.20

i know the difference
between what's real
and a gold-plated friendship.

they both feel like 24 karat
at first but the more
you wear it.
you'll notice the luster fading
day by day

until its golden coat is gone
exposing the pyrite
you fell for.

7.17.18

the chase for your
requited love
intoxicates me more than
any drug ever could

the emotional
firestorm you spark inside of me
burns more than a dirty syringe
piercing through my vein

i'm addicted to the pain you give
i can't feel my chest when
you speak to me

the way you come and go
my heart must be your favorite sport
because you play me every season.

when it's all said and done
you casually leave
without caring about
the casualty you left breathless.

5.5.18

your body is here
but your mind is miles away
in my bed we lay
your thoughts wander
my distant lover.
come closer
i wanna get to know you

message:

don't cling to the idea of receiving closure from the person who hurt you. sometimes there's nothing left to be said, so don't give them a reason to slither back into your life. At the end of the day, *healing is your responsibility.*

Don't Wait til I Die to Love Me III

8:47 pm 2.8.17

after the smoke cleared
i realized you never wanted
me for me

i was your distraction from the past
your rebound, to bounce back

so foolish of me to believe
i could be anything more
than a past time

8:05 pm 2.10.22

all the pictures are gone
and the laughs - faded
but the memories still
the same

i know there's no chance
but i'll be here if you come again

i wish there was a way
to say everything i wanted
before you walked away

i bid you a farewell
wishing you well
it's never easy to move on,
it's even harder to let go

Don't Wait til I Die to Love Me III

10:11 pm 2.10.22

i regret ghosting you,
i hope you have some
forgiveness to spare

i didn't handle your
heart with care
i vanished into thin air

when you confessed
your truest thoughts
i knew i didn't deserve you

i left without a trace
i thought leaving
would be easier than hurting you

10:40 pm 2.9.22

my biggest mistake:

pushing you away
when you just wanted to shed
light on my darkest days

i thought i was doing your heart justice
by setting you free
i feared you'd become imprisoned -
while trying to save me

2:45 pm 3.6.22

after i expressed how I felt
 the words *let's just be friends*
 escaped your breath
i tried to capture those words
and give them back to you.
before they vanished into thin air

after balancing on blurred lines
for so long
one thing became clear
we were on the same page
but different books

when reality pinched,
I failed to change your mind
I came to realize
the friendzone is a waiting room
where love goes to die

note to reader:

as a special thank you, i will send a package of free ebooks to every reader who sends a screenshot of their review via instagram or twitter. please be patient i will respond to your message as soon as possible.

twitter: michaeltavon
ig: bymichaeltavon

the package will include *i am,* a collection of unreleased quotes and affirmations. a collection of poems entitled *love & other things* (written in 2016) and my first novel *garage band* (2013), which is no longer available for sale.

p.s. , follow me on tiktok @michaeltavonpoetry

Made in the USA
Las Vegas, NV
07 November 2024

11311285R00102